Data Analytics for Beginners

Practical Guide To Master Data Analytics

TECHWORLD

© 2017

Respective authors own all copyrights not held by the publisher.

The information herein is offered for informational purposes solely, and is universal as so. The presentation of the information is without contract or any type of guarantee assurance.

The trademarks that are used are without any consent, and the publication of the trademark is without permission or backing by the trademark owner. All trademarks and brands within this book are for clarifying purposes only and are the owned by the owners themselves, not affiliated with this document.

Other Books By **TechWorld**

DevOps Handbook

A Guide to Implementing DevOps In Your Workplace

DevOps is not just a buzzword. It is a mindset that can pull your companies problems by the root and change the traditional, core beliefs. When the old waterfall methods cannot provide you with the desired outcome, it is time for a total transformation that can get you off the downward spiral.

Teaching you the ultimate ways to start implementing DevOps in order to decrease the deployment time and maximize the profit, this book will show you why some of the world's largest companies have chosen to think DevOps.

Introduction

Businesses—whether startups or incumbents—have always had access to data as long as it's available. And strangely enough, these companies have had serious challenges in harnessing their data into meaningful insights in the last few years with the majority of them outsourcing their data analysis functions to expatriates.

Because of skyrocketing volumes of data, today's interest in data analytics is unparalleled. While the previous study centered on a few specific departments, today's analysis has to focus on all the departments of the organization. In particular, the bottom line of enhanced data analytics in these units is improving the performance.

But why now, you may ask?

The global business environment in which the companies are operating from has been changing fast. Really fast! Today's businesses must not only compete to increase their ROI, but they must also face stiff competition from their rivals with limited time to market their services and products. Also, these firms have to put up with the ever-evolving demographics such as the emergence of millennials and web 2.0 technologies.

Amidst all these challenges, data analytics is the only hope for the survival of companies in such business environments. Data analytics generates fact-based and insightful-driven decisions that can help firms manage their strategic, operation and financial performance while creating shareholder value. That's why you can no longer ignore data analytics.

This book has been written to help you understand how data analytics can enable an organization navigates against the turbulences created by challenging and complex business environments. In particular, the book explores all the basics of data analytics and how your business can leverage today's data analytics to promote your bottom line.

Are you ready?

CONTENTS

Chapter 1: Overview of Data Analytics

Welcome to the world of data analytics! In this chapter, we'll explore all the concepts behind data analytics that will help you get started. This section will provide with a complete big picture view of data analytics. Let's dive in.

Foundations of Data Analytics

Today, companies are generating vast amounts of data files. The files are created from multiple sources and exist in different locations across the organization's data storage infrastructure. In some instances, the files can contain structured data which can easily be processed by RDBMSs such as SQL Server, MySQL, and Oracle to generate useful information.

However, in most cases, the files will contain unstructured or semi-structured data in the form of emails, documents and other forms of digital media. Unlike the structured data that can easily be processed, both semi-structured and unstructured data—what is commonly called the big data—are particularly difficult to manipulate. In most cases, the amount of big data created by the organization can not only put a strain on its storage resources but also strain on processing capabilities.

From the storage resource perspective, managing any big data in the organization means locating and removing the files that are:

1

- Obsolete
- Duplicated
- Non-essential

It takes lots of time to search through each of the storage sizes for data that can be archived or even deleted. When you ignore to archive and delete obsolete, duplicated and non-essential files, they will continue to consume your valuable and limited storage capacity.

From the processing resource perspective, manipulating your data requires the application of appropriate statistical skills that can help you mine useful information for decision making. With proper statistical and computing skills, you can quickly evaluate the current state of you data and take actionable steps to help you retrieve and valuable information while mitigating the risk of compliance-related challenges.

Below are benefits that you stand to achieve when you implement best data analytics practices in your organization:

Below are reasons why you should consider investing in data analytics:

- You'll establish a dialogue with your consumers. Today's customers are tough to understand. Data analytics can allow you to profile their clients for a proper understanding of their needs.
- You'll re-examine your products and improve. Data analytics will provide meaningful customers' perception about your product. These sentiments

can help you segment your market based on geographical or time zone requirements.

- You'll be in a position to perform risk analysis with your data. Predictive analysis of your data will enable your firm to data for helpful insights that keep you updated about business environments.
- You'll now generate new revenue streams. You can sell any patterns you obtain from your data to non-personalized large firms and expand your revenue base.

Getting started

By now, you are asking, "Where should I start to become a professional data analyst?"

Good question.

To become a professional data scientist, below are prerequisites:

- Spreadsheets
- Basic SQL
- Web development

Let's see how these fields are important in data analytics.

#1: Spreadsheets

Any spreadsheet such as Ms Excel can help you analyze data. In fact, Ms Excel can be regarded as the most all-around business application that you can use for data analysis. Most of the functional specific skills such as data mining, visualization, and statistical applications are provided in Ms Excel. You can begin by learning the fundamental concepts of Ms Excel such as the workbook, worksheets, formula bar and the ribbon.

If you complete the basics, you can now begin to master the essential functions such as sum, average, if, Vlookup, date, max and getpivotdata. As you become comfortable with these features, you can now dive deeper into more complex formulas for regression, correlation and chi-square distributions.

#2: Basic SQL

Ms Excel will provide you with tools for slicing and dicing your data by assuming that you already have the data stored on your computer. It doesn't provide tools for data collection and storage. As you'll learn about seasoned data analysts, the best approach for dealing with data is pulling it directly from its source which Excel doesn't provide.

Relational database management systems (RDBMS) that use Structured Query Language (SQL) supports procedures that can help you collect and manage your database in an efficient manner. To understand the RDBMSs, you should have an excellent mastery of SQL. You can begin by learning the following SQL statements:

- Select
- From
- Where
- Group By
- Having
- Order By

Besides mastering these SQL commands, you should also find out how primary keys, foreign keys, and candidate keys are used in the RDBMSs.

#3: Basic web development

Oddly enough, web development is a bonus to any data analyst. If you want to work with consumer internet companies such as Microsoft, IBM or Amazon, good internet programming skills in HTML, JavaScript and PHP will help you communicate your results in more effective ways.

Advanced tools and prerequisites for data analytics

If you wish to take your professional career to the next level, then basic pre-requisites for data analytics may be insufficient. Here are advanced tools that can take your career to a new level:

Hadoop

Hadoop is an open-source software framework that stores big data and can allow applications to run on it in the form of clusters. You can use Hadoop to perform highly parallelized operations on your big data. One advantage of Hadoop is that it can allow you to store and process massive storage of data of any type. Because of enormous processing power, Hadoop is suited for analysis of big data with virtually limitless simultaneous tasks.

R programming

Today, there are a couple of programming languages that can perform data analytics. Each of these programming languages has their own fair share of pros and cons. However, R programming language is a tested programming language that you can try out. R is very useful for data analytics due to its versatility nature especially in the field of statistics. It is open source software that provides data scientists with a variety of features for analyzing data.

Below are reasons that make R popular in data analytics:

- It is simple, well developed and one of the dynamic programming languages that support loops recursive functions, conditionals, and input/output facilities.
- It provides programming operators that can perform calculations on vectors, arrays, matrices and lists.
- It has storage facilities, therefore; data analysts can effectively handle their data.
- It has graphical facilities that data analysts can use to display processed data.

Python programming
Python is a very powerful, open source and flexible programming language that is easy to learn, use and has perfect libraries for data manipulation, management, and analysis. Its simple syntax is easy to learn and resembles MatLab, C or C++ or Java. If you have basic skills in these programming languages, you'll not have a problem with Python language.

Also, Python combines the features of general-purpose

programming language and those of analytical and quantitative computing. In the recent past, Python has been applied in scientific computing with highly quantitative domains. For instance, Python has found its applications in finance, physics, oil, gas and signal processing.

Similarly, Python has been used to develop popular scalable web applications such as YouTube. Because of its popularity, Python can help you with tools for big data and business analytics in science, engineering and other areas of scalable computing. You can use Python's inbuilt libraries such as Panda and NumPy to help you with data analytics.

MatLab
MATLAB is a high-performance language that is meant for technical computing. It easily integrates the computation, visualization, and programming in an environment where problems and solutions can be expressed in a conversant programming notation. MATLAB is a collaborate language whose basic data component is an array that does not require any dimensioning.

This allows a data scientist to solve many technical computing problems, especially those that can be modeled in in matrix and vector formats. MatLab can be used in the following areas:

- Data exploration, analysis, and visualization
- Mathematics and computation
- Development of algorithm

- Modeling, prototyping, and simulation
- Scientific and engineering graphics

Perl

Perl is a dynamic and high-level programming language that you can use for data analytics. Originally developed as a scripting language for UNIX by Larry Wall, Perl has provided its UNIX-like features and flexibility of any programming language to develop robust and scalable systems.

With the advent of the internet in 1990's, Perl usage exploded. Besides providing dominant features of CGI programming, Perl has also become an essential language for data analysis because of its comprehensive set of analysis libraries.

Mathematics and Analysis

The fact is: data analytics is all about numbers. If you fancy working with numbers and algebraic functions, then data analytics is for you. If you don't love numbers, then it's time to begin developing a positive attitude. You should be willing to learn new ideas. As a matter of fact, data analytics is ever-changing and fast-paced, thanks to the exponential growth of data and IT capabilities.

Analysis and Analytics

Even though Analysis and Analytics sound similar in pronunciation, there's an important distinction between the two terms. Analysis can be regarded as the discipline of recognizing the business needs of the organization and determining their solutions. On the other hand,

8

Analytics focuses on data collection, techniques, and skills that can help in the investigation of past business performance.

In particular, the primary role of Analysis is to separate the whole business problem into its parts while analytics provide a logical solution to the problems identified in the organization. When you think regarding the past and future, the analysis looks backward over the time and gives you a historical view of what has happened in the organization while analytics models the future or predict the result.

Communicating Data Insights

Data flows everywhere in the organization. But, consuming and communicating the data insights is no easy task. Once your company starts collecting and combining all kinds of data, the next step which can be elusive is extracting value from it. Your data can hold incredible amounts of potential value, but not an ounce of any value can be generated unless insights are uncovered and translated into business outcomes or actions.

These days, you can use a variety of new tools to communicate the results of your analytics. Obviously, the choice of your communication tool will depend on the situation and your audience. It is a fact that visual analytics—also called data visualization—has dramatically advanced communication of data insights. Below are some of the typical visual analytics:

- Bar graphs

- Pie charts
- Line charts
- Scatter graphs

Ideally, the use of bar graphs, pie charts, line charts and scatter graphs can only scratch the surface of whatever you want to do with the visual display. More advanced visual display tools such as matrix plots, heat maps, bubble charts, and treemaps can provide more options for displaying the data insights.

With several data visualization tools, it can be challenging at some point to settle a particular method. In such a case, you can employ more advanced customized tools such as SAS Visual Analytics, Games and Gapminder to help you communicate your data insights effectively.

Chapter 2: Basics of Data Analytics

Data analytics is a diverse subject matter. In part, this is because data analytics represent a broad range of disciplines, including (but not limited to) statistics, computer science and even communication. Furthermore, within each discipline, data analytics can use some different methodologies such as Quantitative and Qualitative Approaches to undertaking analytics.

Despite this diversity in methodologies, data analytics share some common characteristics. In this chapter, we delve deeper to provide you with a complete big picture view of data analytic basics. Are you ready?

Planning a study

Just like any research process, proper planning is required for an effective data analytics process. The concrete steps that you'll follow during the planning phase will depend, in part, on the problem to be investigated in the organization, availability of data analytic tools and a host of other factors. Nonetheless, it is precise to say that much of data analytics will follow the systematic course of actions.

Below are questions that you should ask yourself at the planning stage:

- What is the problem that needs to be investigated in the organization?
- How will data be collected?

- Which are data analytic tools available for data analysis?

Answering the above questions will provide you with a roadmap for your data analytic process. Next up, you should proceed to the data collection stage.

Surveys

Flawed data can guide even the greatest data analytics in the wrong directions. You should be absolutely sure that you're getting the accurate data using the right methods. Surveys can have a significant impact on the direction of your company when it comes to data analytics. Before creating your survey, it's vital to think about its objective. The common goals of most surveys include:

- Compiling the market research in your organization
- Soliciting feedback from your customers
- Monitoring the performance of your organization

For you to design a proper survey, you should note down the specific knowledge that you'd like to gain from the survey along with the problems that you had identified during the planning stage.

Next up, identify the answers to the questions that you'd like to answer and write down the percentage of the responses that you would like to get from the data analytics. Comparing the future results against your expectation will provide the best guess on how you'll proceed with data analysis.

The pre-survey process will also help you to synthesize

the important aspects of the survey process and guide you through the design process. Always remember that the larger scope the survey will reduce the number of respondents that can take participate in the survey.

Also, the manner in which you structure your questions and answers will help define the limits of the analysis when you summarize the results. The four primary response data types should guide you when structuring your questions:

- **_Categorical data_**. These include unordered labels such as colors or brand names. This is the simplest type of data that can help you analyze data because you'll only be limited to calculating the share of the responses in each category.
- **_Ordinal_**. These will provide you with a Likert scale with labels such as "Strongly Disagree" and "Strongly Agree."
- **_Interval_**. It will help you structured questions that include ranges such as "Number of employees."
- **_Ratio_**. It will help you structure issues such as "Inches of rain."

Experiments
The experimental data is generated from a measurement, test method or experimental design. For instance, you can use an experimental design to produce results in clinical trials experiment. Experimental data can either be qualitative or quantitative with each discipline focusing on different investigations.

In an experiment, you'll attempt to observe the results of the experiment conducted intentionally so that you discover useful insights from it or demonstrate a known fact. With an experiment, you'll be able to draw conclusions concerning that factor of the study group as you make inferences from a sample to the larger population of interest. When designed correctly, an experiment can help you establish a cause-and-effect relationship between different variables.

Gathering Data

Gathering data is the process of collecting and measuring information on the targeted variables based on established systematic fashion that allows you to answer basic questions about your analytic process. Ms Excel is familiar and easy-to-use software that can help you collect and manipulate data. When using Excel to gather data, you should know how to use the tables.

This process begins by setting up an appropriate data preparation.

During data preparation, the rule of thumb in using Excel is setting up the data table.

Setting up the Excel table

Organizing Ms Excel data table can save you lots of time during data analytics. Basically, Ms Excel table is arranged in rows and columns. Each row represents one chunk of data. In RDBMSs terminologies, this is what forms one record. Depending on the nature of your Excel table, a record can be the customer's contact information or the invoice data.

Columns hold one type of data for each record. In RDBMSs terminologies, this is what forms one field. For instance, if your Ms Excel table contains data about customers, then one field can be the client name while another one can be the client address of the customer and so on. The first row of the Excel table should usually is reserved for the column headers. It is at the row headers that you will place field names such as "Customer Name" and "Customer Address." Ms Excel uses these names as the labels for the data entry form.

Here are tips for effective Ms Excel data structure:

- All the data should be entered in a single spreadsheet file.
- Always enter variable names in the first row of the spreadsheet file.
- The variable names should not be longer than eight characters and should start with a letter.
- The variable names should not contain spaces. However, they can start with an underscore character.
- There should be no other text rows such as the titles in the spreadsheet.
- There should be no blank rows appearing in the Excel data.
- If you have multiple groups of data, place them in the same spreadsheet together with variable names that show group membership.
- Avoid using the alphabetic characters for values.
- If your data group has two levels such as Male or Female, coding them using 0 and 1 makes sense

as it allows easier analysis.

- For missing data values, always leave the cell blank.
- It is a good practice to enter dates using the slashes such as 5/05/2017) and the times with colons such as (12:15 AM).

Now, keying data into the worksheet and moving the cursor after each and every entry can be frustrating. Fortunately, Ms Excel has data entry forms that can ease your pain. With only a sprint of the setup and knowledge of forms, Ms Excel can fast-track the process of data collection when you use the forms. After setting up your Ms Excel table, you should now proceed to set up Ms Excel form that will help you to capture the data.

Setting up the Excel Form

The following are steps that will help you configure an Excel data form:

- Highlight the entire data and click on the Home ribbon.
- While on the Home ribbon, Click on Table, and select any one of the table styles that you see. With this done, you're now ready to set up your form.

Now ensure you have displayed the Forms Button. If you're using Excel 2007, the Forms Button will not be available. For you to view it use the Quick Access Menu to add it or follow the following steps:

- Right-click any empty space on the Excel ribbon

and select *"Customize the Ribbon."*

- In the dialog box that shows up, set "Choose commands from:" to choose Commands that are not in the Ribbon.
- On the right-hand of the Excel Window, select Data and click on the *"New Group"* button.
- On the left-hand side of the Window, click "Form..."
- Finally, with both the "Form..." and New Group (Custom) highlighted, click the Add >> button.

With this done, you can now set up your form.

The headers that you will have specified in the top row of the Excel table will now be the field names. By default, the dialog box that crops us when you fire the Form Wizard shows the first existing record that you had entered in your table. You can browse and change the current records as you wish with the "Find Next" and "Find Prep" buttons.

To add another record or row to Excel table, just click the "New" button. When you're done, click the "Close" button. This way, you'll find the process of data entry using Excel much simpler than you thought.

Selecting a useful sample

The process of data analysis begins with identifying the population from which you'll obtain data. Because it's practically impossible to get data on every subject in the population, you should use an appropriate sampling technique to get a sample size that's representative. A typical statistical process is a four-step phase activity that includes the following:

- Estimate the expected proportion of the population that you want to study. The proportion of that population must of interest to the study.
- Determine the confidence interval for use in your analysis. Think of confidence level as the "margin of error" in your sample size. Now, all the empirical estimates are based on a sample that must have a certain degree of uncertainty. It's a must for you to specify the desired total spectrum of the confidence interval.
- Set the value of the confidence level. This provides the precision or level of uncertainty in the analysis. A narrow confidence interval that has a high confidence level such as 99% is likely to be as representative of the entire population as possible.
- Determine the sample size. Samples are often too large. This can waste time, resources and money using them as the basis for data analytics. On the other hand, when the sample size is too small, it can lead to inaccurate results. If you know the confidence level and the population size, you can use a statistical table to estimate your sample size. If the number that is required is too large, you can recalculate it with lower confidence levels or use wider intervals to choose a smaller sample size.

Avoiding bias in a data set

Bias in any data set is a mortal enemy of both experimental and survey research. Therefore, it's important to guard against any biases that may arise in a data set. Bias can occur during the planning, data collection, analytics, and even publication stages of the research. Understanding biases in data sets can allow you to critically and independently review all data analytic literature.

A thorough knowledge of bias in datasets and how it impacts the analytic results is essential for the practice of evidence-based decision making in organizations. Bias in data sets can be categorized into the following groups:

- Pre-trial bias. The sources of the pre-trial bias include errors from the study design and in respondents' recruitment causing fatal flaws in the results of the analytics which can't be compensated during data analysis. These errors can be avoided by careful selection of the sample size and wording of the questions to be used in the analytics.
- Bias during data collection. These are errors that occur in measurements of any exposure or outcomes. For instance, the information obtained and recorded from respondents in different study groups may be different. To avoid such errors, the data collection instruments have to be cleaned to ensure they are valid and reliable.

- Bias during publication phase. Some errors may occur during the presentation of the study results. For instance, citation and confounding errors can happen at the publication stage of the analytics process. To curb these mistakes, the data must be tested for reliability and validity to ensure it conforms to the problem at hand.

Explaining Data

We have so far explored an overview of data analytics and the central concepts behind data analytics. But even before we proceed, let's start off by answering the question: "What is data?"

Well, the word data conjures different meanings depending on the context in which it is used. In measurements or statistics, data can be viewed as factual information that forms the foundations of reasoning, discussion, and calculations. In a sense, we can use data to provide facts about the performance of an organization or the economic growth of a country.

In computer science, data refers to raw facts such as numbers, characters, images that can be captured by any method of recording. These raw facts are meaningless when presented to users. For them to be meaningful, they have to be processed into information. It is the information that helps firms to make decisions about some action.

The majority of people believe that data has no meaning until it's interpreted or processed to make it meaningful. Whenever we carefully examine data to find out patterns in it for significant decisions to be made, we're actually using it as a component that generates knowledge. In understanding what data entails, it's vital to know that it can be collected in any form. It could be in numbers, pictures, maps, words or even in newspaper articles.

I know you're asking: "Which data format is better?"

Well, all the formats are better depending on what you would like to analyze. Ideally, the type of data that you'll be dealing with will be either qualitative or quantitative.

Qualitative data

Data is said to be qualitative if it can be described in words. In other words, whatever you observe in the data is what you'll record. The observation can be based on color observations, odor or even texture.

For instance, suppose you are a marine biologist studying the behavior and the activities of dolphins. Surely, you will be identifying different dolphins within the group and observing them on a frequent basis. If you are recording their detailed observations, then the following will form the qualitative data.

- The colors of dolphin range from gray to white.
- When placed in a pod, the dolphins engage in play behavior.
- Dolphins have smooth skins

Quantitative data

The data that we say is quantitative must have numeric measurements. Ideally, such data must be objective. By objective, I mean that the data must be the same regardless of who measures it. For instance, in qualitative data, different people can observe different colors for the same dolphin if one is a color blind.

However, in quantitative data, it must be the same. For instance, measurements such as length, mass, temperature, time, concentration and frequency will always be objective. Going back to our earlier example of research on dolphin, the following are examples of quantitative data that you can collect:

- There are thirteen dolphins in the pod.
- Dolphins eat an equivalent of 10-12% of their body mass each day.
- The sonar frequency that dolphins use is approximately 100 kHz.

Now that you understand what data entails let's examine the importance of data analytics to businesses.

Descriptive Analytics

Statistics can be grouped into two broad categories namely descriptive and inferential statistics. The primary function of descriptive analytics is to summarize the data based on what has happened in the organization. It examines the raw data or content to provide answers to the following questions:

- What happened?
- What is happening?

In particular, descriptive analytics provides brief and summarized descriptively for a given data set, which can be a representational—if the sample size was used—or the entire population if the census method was used to study the population. Think of descriptive statistics as that branch of statistics which analyzes a big chunk of data to provide summarized charts using descriptive measures such as:

- The measures of central tendency such as mean, mode, and median.
- The measures of dispersion such as range, variance, and standard deviation.
- The measures of a shape such as skewness and kurtosis.

Descriptive analytics are usually broken down into measures of the central tendency and measures of the variability. When you use descriptive analytics to summarize your data, the following data visualization tools can help you communicate the results:

- Bar graphs
- Pie charts
- Line charts
- Scatter graphs
- Bubble graphs
- Treemaps

Chapter 3: Descriptive Statistics

Descriptive statistics is that branch of statistics that provides brief and summarized descriptively for a given data set, which can be a representational—if the sample size was used—or the entire population if the census method was used to study the population. It is usually grouped into two broad categories:

- Measures of central tendency
- Measures of dispersion
- Measures of shape

Measures of central tendency

These measures try to describe a data set by identifying the core position within that data set. Intrinsically, measures of central tendency—which are sometimes called measures of central location—provides a single score that best describes the entire data distribution.

The common examples of measures of central tendency are:

- The mean
- The mode
- The median

In this chapter, we explore the measures of central tendency to provide you with an understanding of how to use each of them. Let's dive in.

The mean

The mean—or the average— is the most popular and well-known measure of central tendency. The mean can be used with both discrete and continuous data. The mean is equivalent to the sum of all values in the data set divided by some values in the data set. For instance, if you're given n values in a data set of X_1, $X_2...X_n$, then the mean can be given as:

$$\bar{x} = \frac{(x_1 + x_2 + \cdots + x_n)}{n}$$

The above formula can also be re-written as:

$$\bar{x} = \frac{\sum x}{n}$$

The mean is, in essence, a model of your entire dataset. It is the value with the most common in most data distributions. It tries to minimize errors in the prediction of any one value that is present in your data set. By this I mean the value that produces the lowest amount of error from all the other values in the given data set.

However, the mean has one main flaw: it is susceptible to the influence of the outliers. In some datasets, there may be values that are unusual compared to the rest of the data set by either being too small or too large. Consider the table below:

Staff	1	2	3	4	5	6	7	8	9	10
Salary	15k	18k	16k	14k	15k	15k	12k	17k	90k	95k

The mean salary for the ten staff is $30.7k. Now, by inspecting the raw data set, you can realize that the mean value isn't the best way to accurately demonstrate the typical salary of any worker since the majority of workers has salaries in the range of $12k to 18k. Therefore, we can say the two large salaries have skewed the mean.

The median

The median is the middle score for any data set which has been arranged in order of magnitude. Unlike mean, the median is less affected by the outliers and skewed data. Consider the table below:

65	55	89	56	35	14	56	55	87	45	92

To compute the median, we have to arrange the data set from smallest data value to the largest data value or vice versa. Here is what we get when we organize the data set from smallest value to the largest value:

14	35	45	55	55	56	56	65	87	89	92

Note that our table has 11 data elements. Therefore the middle value is the sixth term which can be obtained by the formula:

Median term= $(n+1)/2$

Is 56. 56 is the median value there are 5 scores before it and 5 other scores after it.

The mode

It is the frequent score in any given dataset. If you're using a histogram, the mode will represent the highest bar in the bar chart or the histogram.

Chapter 4: Measures of Dispersion

The measures of dispersion—also called measures of variability, scatter, or the spread—are descriptive statistical measures that determine the extent to which a given data distribution is stretched or squeezed. The most common examples of measures of statistical dispersion are:

- The variance
- The standard deviation
- The coefficient of variation

This chapter explores the measures of dispersion to provide you with an understanding of how to use each of them. Let's dive in.

The variance

The variance—which is abbreviated as σ^2—is a measure of how far each data value in the data set is from the mean. To calculate the σ^2 of a given data set, follow the procedures below:

- Compute the average of the data set.
- Deduct the mean from each data value in the set. This provides you with a measure of the distance of each data value from the mean.
- Square each of these distances—to obtain all positive values—and sum all of the squares together.
- Divide the sum of the squares by the total number of values in the data set.

Mathematically, the variance of a given data set can be defined as:

$$\sigma^2 = \frac{\sum (X - \mu)^2}{N}$$

Note in the above formula that the variance is simply the sum of the squared distances of each data value in the distribution from the mean (μ), divided by the total number of terms in the distribution (N).

As an example, consider the example below:

Let's go back to the two distributions that we started looked at in our first example.

Dataset 1: 3, 4, 4, 5, 6, 8

Dataset 2: 1, 2, 4, 5, 7, 11

Suppose we want to compute the variance of each data set, we'll first construct a table that calculates the values. Here is how the table will appear after taking into consideration all the terms in the formula for computing variance:

Dataset	N	ΣX	ΣX^2	M	μ^2	σ^2
1	6	30	166	5	25	2.67
2	6	30	216	5	25	11

Even though both the data sets have the same mean (μ = 5), the variance (σ^2) of the second data set is 11.00, which is a little more than four times the variance of the first data set at 2.67.

The standard deviation

The standard deviation is the square root of the variance. Here are steps that you can follow when computing the standard deviation:

- Calculate the mean of the data set.
- Deduct the average from each data value in the set. This provides you with a measure of the distance of each data value from the mean.
- Square each of these distances—to obtain all positive values—and sum all of the squares together.
- Divide the sum of the squares by the total number of values in the data set.
- Find the square root of the sum of the sum of squares divided by the total number of data values.

Mathematically, the standard deviation of a data set can be defined as follows:

$$\sigma = \sqrt{\frac{1}{N}\sum_{i=1}^{N}(x_i - \mu)^2}$$

Let's now use our previous example on variance to compute the variance. We have two data sets:

Dataset 1: 3, 4, 4, 5, 6, 8

Dataset 2: 1, 2, 4, 5, 7, 11.

We'll proceed and construct the table as follows:

Dataset	N	ΣX	ΣX^2	M	μ^2	σ^2	σ
1	6	30	166	5	25	2.67	
2	6	30	216	5	25	11	

Note that we have now added an extra column for standard deviation. To compute the values of σ, we'll simply get the square root of σ.

Here's how the table appears after getting the square roots of the variance:

Dataset	N	ΣX	ΣX^2	M	μ^2	σ^2	σ
1	6	30	166	5	25	2.67	1.63
2	6	30	216	5	25	11	3.32

Coefficients of Variation

The Coefficient of Variation (CV) defines the amount of variability relative to the mean. Since the CV is unit-less, you can use it instead of the standard deviation when you want to compare the spread of data sets that have different units or even various means.

For instance, you are the quality control examiner at milk bottle manufacturing plant that bottles small and large containers. You take a sample of each milk product and observe that the mean volume of the smaller containers is 1 cup with a standard deviation of 0.08. You also find out that the average volume of the large containers is 1 gallon or 16 with a standard deviation of 0.4.

You can note that the standard deviation of the gallon container is nearly five times greater that of the smaller containers. However, when you compute their CVs, you'll find out a different measure. For instance, the CVs is:

Larger container	Smaller container
CV = 100 x 0.4 / 16 = 2.50	CV = 100 x 0.08/ 1 = 8

The CV of the small container (8) is more than three times greater than the CV of the large container (2.5). In other words, even though the large container has a higher standard deviation, the smaller bottle has more variability relative to its mean.

Chapter 5: Measures of shape

A fundamental process in the majority of data analytics is to characterize the location and the variability of a data set. A further characterization of the datasets includes skewness and kurtosis. Measures of shape—or measures of symmetry—are used to characterize location and variability of a statistical dataset.

But what do these terminologies mean?

Let's begin by skewness.

Skewness

Skewness is a measure of shape or symmetry, or more precisely, lack of symmetry. A statistical distribution, or data set, is only symmetric if it looks the same to the Left-side and right-side of the center point. In other words, skewness is the asymmetry in any statistical distribution, where the curve appears distorted or skewed either to the left side or the right side.

We can look at skewness as the extent to which a statistical distribution differs from the normal distribution. For any univariate data Y_1, Y_2... Y_N, the formula for skewness can be given as:

$$g1 = \frac{\sum Ni=1 (Yi - Y^-)^3 / N}{s^3}$$

In the above expression, Y^- is the mean, s is the standard deviation, and N is the number of the data points. The skewness of any normal distribution is always zero, while any symmetric data set should have its skewness near zero. The negative values of skewness imply that the data is skewed left and while positive values for the skewness mean that the data is skewed right.

By being skewed left, we mean that the left-tail of the data is long relative to the right-tail. Similarly, being skewed right means that the right-tail of the dataset is long relative to the left-tail. Some statistical measurements that have a lower bound may be skewed right. For instance, in reliability studies, the failure times can't be negative.

Kurtosis

Kurtosis is a measure of whether the statistical data is heavy-tailed or light-tailed relative to the normal distribution. Therefore, datasets with high kurtosis tend to be heavy-tailed or have outliers. On the other hand, the data sets that have low kurtosis tend to be light-tailed or lack the outliers. Similarly, a uniform distribution would be the extreme case.

A histogram is a perfect graphical technique for demonstrating both the skewness and kurtosis of statistical datasets. For any univariate data Y_1, Y_2... Y_N, the formula for kurtosis can be given as:

$$g1 = \frac{\sum N i = 1 (Y i - Y^-)^4 / N}{s^4}$$

In the above expression, Y^- is the mean, s is the standard deviation, and N is the number of the data points. Many conventional statistical tests and intervals rely on the normality assumptions. Any significant skewness and kurtosis clearly show that datasets are not normal. If the data set exhibits significant skewness or kurtosis, then you can apply a transformation to make it normal or nearly normal.

You can also use techniques that are based on distributions other than the normal distributions. For instance, in reliability studies, you can use exponential, Weibull, and even lognormal distributions to model the data and make it normal rather than using the normal distribution. In that case, your probability plot correlation coefficient and the probability plot will be necessary when determining a good distributional model for your dataset.

Drawing conclusions

Both variance and standard deviation provide a numerical measure of scattering for a given data set. These measures are helpful when making comparisons between data sets that go beyond the simple visual impressions. The standard deviation can be difficult to interpret if it is presented as a single number. However, a smaller value for standard deviation implies that the values in the dataset are close to the mean of the data set.

On the other hand, a large standard deviation suggests that the values in the statistics set are farther away from the average. A smaller value for the standard deviation can be a goal in certain scenarios where the results are restricted, for instance, in the product manufacturing and quality control systems. A particular type of vehicle part that has to be 3 centimeters in diameter to fit properly had better not have a large standard deviation during the construction process.

On the other hand, a large standard deviation in such a scenario would imply that lots of vehicle parts will end up in the trash since they don't fit properly. But in situations where you just observe and record statistical data, a large standard deviation may not necessarily be a bad thing since it just shows a significant amount of variation in the group of elements that are being studied.

For instance, when you look at salaries for every employee of a particular company ranging from the student intern to the CEO, you may find that the standard deviation may be significant. When you narrow down the group by examining only the student interns, you'll find out that the standard deviation is smaller. This is because the individuals within such a group will always have salaries that are less variable.

What about skewness and kurtosis?

Skewness can be viewed as the extent to which a statistical distribution differs from the normal distribution. Therefore, a zero skewness value means that the distribution is normal. Similarly, any symmetric data set that has a near zero value means that the dataset is normal. The negative values of skewness imply that the data is skewed left and while positive values for the skewness mean that the data is skewed right.

When the value of skewness is negative, it means that the left-tail of the data is long relative to the right-tail. On the other hand, a positive value means that the right-tail of the dataset is long relative to the left-tail. Some statistical measurements that have a lower bound may be skewed right such as reliability studies; where the failure times can't be negative.

Kurtosis, on the other hand, determines whether the statistical data is heavy-tailed or light-tailed relative to the normal distribution. In particular datasets with high kurtosis tend be heavy-tailed, or have outliers while data sets that have low kurtosis tend to be light-tailed or lack the outliers.

Chapter 6: Charts and Graphs

Ms Excel provides an excellent range of great charts that can help visualize your data. You can exploit these full ranges of visualization tools to help you explore your data and create reports that have color-coded data values with interactive slicers. The following guidelines should be considered when visualizing data in Ms Excel:

Always use the Power View when exploring data with a range of data visualizations. The Power View is vital when you want to establish relationships between data that exists in multiple tables.

You can use the Power Map to show the changes in geographically-related dispersed data values over a given time.

Use the native Pivot Charts and the conditional formatting when creating data visualizations in workbooks that will be launched in versions of Excel that don't support Power View or the Power Map.

Below are common tools that you can use to visualize the data:

- Pie charts
- Bar graphs
- Time charts
- Line graphs
- Histograms
- Scatter plots

Let's jump in to explore how these data visualization tools can help you during analytics.

#1: **Pie charts**

For you want to visualize data in the form of slices to the total value or pie, then you should consider using pie charts. Pie charts usually display the contribution of each value—or the slice—to a total (pie). Pie charts rely on one data series. Here is an example:

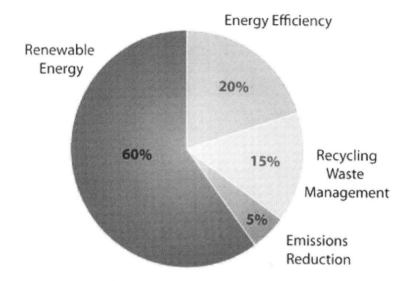

Here are steps that you should follow if you want to create a pie chart in Ms Excel:

Step One: Type your data into the Microsoft Excel worksheet. You can begin by typing your categories in one column and the numbers in a second column. Don't leave blank rows or columns when typing data in the Excel sheet.

Step two: Highlight the data you've just entered. To highlight the data, click on the top left of your data and then drag the mouse cursor to the bottom right.

Step three: Click on "Insert," followed by "Pie," and then click the type of pie chart you want from the menu that appears. If you want a simple pie chart such as the one shown above, a 2D selection will work fine. Once you have clicked on the chart icon, Ms Excel will automatically insert the pie chart into your worksheet.

If you made a mistake your data entries, you don't have to start afresh. Just type your correction in the original data and Ms Excel will automatically update the pie chart.

#2: Bar graphs

They display information in the form of horizontal or vertical rectangular bars. The bars levels off the appropriate level to define values on the plane. Below is an example:

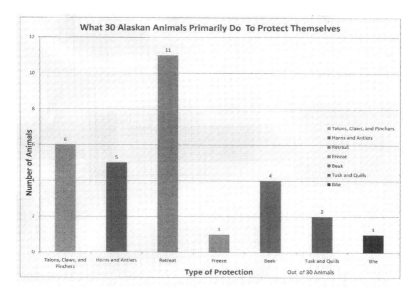

Here are quick steps that can help you create a bar graph in Ms Excel:

Step One: Type your data into the Microsoft Excel worksheet. You can begin by typing your categories in one column and the numbers in a second column. Don't leave blank rows or columns when typing data in the Excel sheet.

Step two: Highlight the data you've just entered. To highlight the data, click on the top left of your data and then drag the mouse cursor to the bottom right.

Step three: Click on "Insert," followed by "Bar," and then click the type of pie chart you want from the menu that appears. If you want a simple pie chart such as the one shown above, a 2D selection will work fine. Once you have clicked on the chart icon, Ms Excel will automatically insert the pie chart into your worksheet.

Step Four: Switch the axes, if necessary by clicking on "Axes" on the Ribbon and typing the labels for axes.

Step five: Adjust your labels and legends, if desired by clicking on "Labels and Legends" on the Ribbon and typing in the appropriate labels.

If you made a mistake your data entries, you don't have to start afresh. Just type your correction in the original data and Ms Excel will automatically update the pie chart.

#3: Time charts

A time series chart—also called times series graph—is an illustration of the data points at successive time intervals. A time chart can help evaluate patterns and behavior in data over a given time. It usually displays the observations on the y-axis against the equally spaced time intervals on the x-axis. Here's an example:

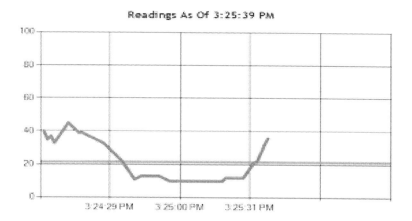

#4: Line Graphs

The line graphs are used to compare changes that take place over the same period for more than one group of data. Here is an example:

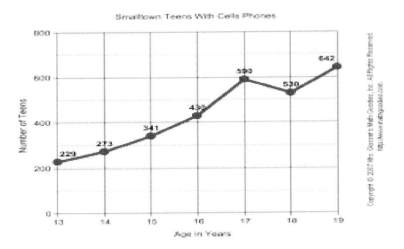

Here are quick steps that you should follow if you want to create a line chart in Ms Excel:

Step One: Type your data into the Microsoft Excel worksheet. You can begin by typing your categories in one column and the numbers in a second column. Don't leave blank rows or columns when typing data in the Excel sheet.

Step two: Highlight the data you've just entered. To highlight the data, click on the top left of your data and then drag the mouse cursor to the bottom right.

Step three: Click on "Insert," followed by "Line," and then click the type of line chart you want from the menu that appears.

If you made a mistake your data entries or you want to insert another set of data you don't have to start afresh. Just type your correction in the original data or add the extra data in the rows and columns you had created, and Ms Excel will automatically update the pie chart.

#5: **Histograms**

A histogram—also called a frequency polygon—is a graph formed by joining of the midpoints of histogram column tops. The histograms are used when depicting data from the continuous variables. Below is an example of a histogram:

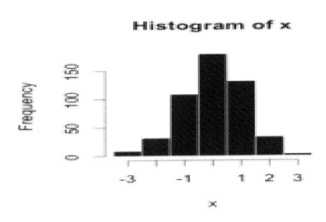

Here are steps to follow when creating a histogram in Ms Excel:

Step one: Load the Data Analysis Toolpak, if it hasn't been installed. To confirm if the Toolpak is installed, click on the "Data" tab and check the far right. When you see Data Analysis, then the Toolpak is installed. If it hasn't been installed, click on "File" followed by "Option." In the menu that appears, click on "Analysis Toolpak" and follow the onscreen instructions to install it.

Step two: Enter the data into a single column of your Excel sheet. For instance, type your values into column A.

Step three: Enter your BINs (Boundary intervals) into a single column (for example, column B) For example, if you have data sets 0-10, 11-20 and 21-30 you can enter 10, 20, 30 in column B.

Step Four: Click the *"Data"* tab and then click the *"Data Analysis"* button.

Step five: Select *"Histogram"* and then click the "OK" button.

Step six: Type the location of your data in Input Range Box that appears. For instance, if your data is in cells A3 to A13 then type A3: A13 into the box.

Step Seven: Type the location of the BINS into the *"Bin Range"* input box. For example, type "B3: B13" into the input box to indicate your BINS are in cells B3 to B13.

Step Eight: Select the option the location of your histogram.

Step Nine: Check the "Chart Output" input box. If you don't check this, you will only get a frequency chart and not the actual histogram.

Step ten: Click on the "OK" button, and Ms Excel will create the histogram.

#6: Scatter plots

The scatter plots are similar to the line graphs because they also use the horizontal and vertical axes to plot data points. However, scatterplots have a very specific purpose—to show how much one variable is affected or is related to another or correlation. Here is an example:

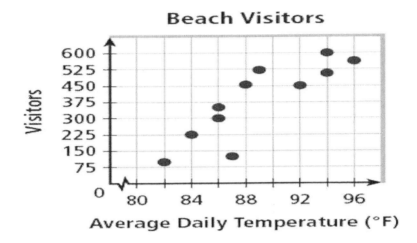

Here are quick steps for creating scatterplots in Ms Excel:

Step One: Type your data into the Microsoft Excel worksheet. You can begin by typing your categories in one column and the numbers in a second column. Don't leave blank rows or columns when typing data in the Excel sheet.

Step two: Highlight the data you've just entered.

Step three: Click on "Insert," followed by "Scatter," and then click the type of scatter chart you want from the menu that appears. If you want a simple pie chart such as the one shown above, a 2D selection will work fine.

Once you have clicked on the chart icon, Ms Excel will automatically insert the scatterplot into your worksheet.

If you made a mistake your data entries, you don't have to start afresh. Just type your correction in the original data and Ms Excel will automatically update the pie chart.

Chapter 7: Application of Data Analytics to Business and Industry

The bottom line of any data analytic process is unearthing the "hidden" value in data sets. In particular, data Analytics applies both statistical and logical techniques to describe, condense and evaluate raw data with the goal of unraveling insightful information that can aid in decision making. This chapter explores the applications of data analytics to businesses and the industry.

Business Intelligence

Business intelligence (BI) combines data warehousing, predictive business analytics, business strategies, performance and user interface to help organizations attain a strategic competitive advantage. The BI applications receive data from the internal and external environment and organize it into a form suitable for utilization in the organization.

Business Intelligence can be used for the following business purposes to drive business value:

- Measurement. The BI program can create a hierarchy of performance metrics and other benchmarking tools that informs the top management about the progress towards business goals.
- Analytics. The BI program can develop quantitative processes for a business to achieve

optimal decisions and to perform business knowledge discovery parameters. This can incorporate data mining, predictive analytics, statistical analysis, predictive modeling and business process modeling.

- Enterprise Reporting. Bi can create an infrastructure for data visualization to help in strategic reporting for the firm.
- Knowledge Management. Bi can make the company data-driven using strategies and practices that identify, creates, represent, and distribute the adoption of insights and experiences that are true business knowledge.

Applications of Business Intelligence

As the importance of BI continues to grow, organizations are finding more and more applications for Business Intelligence. Here are some applications of BI in organizations:

- Banking. BI systems are used in banks to predict the customers' ability to be advanced loans. The BI applications can determine whether a customer's credit rating is "good" or "bad" based on parameters such as age, current savings, and income.
- Supply chain management. When applied in supply chain and management, BI can scale up internal efficiencies to allow organizations use their operational data for trend analysis and craft better business strategies to achieve profitability.
- Manufacturing. The BI software can sift through

large sets data from across the supply chain and provide insightful information to the company for better decisions about managing inventories.

- Public sector. BI can help governments design fraud detection systems and personnel attrition.
- Healthcare. BI is a must-implement solution for healthcare providers that want to standardize data, reduce healthcare data redundancy and costs while complying with industry standards for enhanced efficiencies.
- Customer Relationship Management. BI platforms can consolidate data into a central place to allow organizations improve and expand their existing relationships about improving customer service using historical data on all the previous customer interactions.

Data analytics in business and industry

Across all the industries, big data and advanced analytics are helping businesses to become smarter and better at making predictions that are improving productivity. Today, most companies have recognized that they have opportunities to use big data and analytics to raise their productivity, improve decision making, and gain a strategic competitive advantage. Here are reasons why data analytics has become a buzzword in the majority of organizations:

- Data analytics provides large statistical samples that enhance analytic tool results. The majority of tools that are designed for data mining tend to be optimized for large data sets providing firms with the abilities to deal with large sets of data.

- Analytic tools and databases can now handle big data by executing large queries and parse tables in record time. The recent generations of vendor-specific tools and platforms have increased the rate information flow in organizations allowing them to make prompt decisions.

- Big data is vital in leveraging with analytics. The new technologies and best practices have improved processing capabilities allowing organizations to harness archive data to helpful insights.

Chapter 8: Data Mining

The ever-increasing volumes of data that is being generated each year are making the process of extracting useful information more complex and challenging. Data that is frequently stored in the data warehouse, a repository of data collected from various sources such as corporate databases and summarized data from internal systems and external sources.

For such data, analytics includes simple processing such as querying and reporting, statistical analysis and more complex data mining to derive useful and hidden insights. But what is the difference between data analytics and data mining? This chapter will explain the fundamental differences between these two terminologies and provide you with a big picture view of data mining.

Differences between data analytics and data mining

If you are a newbie in this industry, you may get confused and think data analytics and data mining similar. Trust me; these two terminologies are as cheese and chalks.

Let me begin with data analytics:

Data analytics is the process of exploring the facts from data with specifics of answering particular organizational questions. The techniques that you use in data analytics will be the same as those employed in BI. You should use various tools to get the right data analytics, such as data visualization tools and the right frameworks such as Ms Excel, Python or R.

What about data mining?

Data mining is a process that you can use to structure your raw data and formulate various patterns using mathematical and computational algorithms. At the outset, data mining is useful when you want to generate new information and unlock the different hidden insights. First, the data placed into a data warehouse that performs the required extraction of data to generate meaningful relationships and patterns. There are several mining techniques that you can apply to data while in the warehouse to extract meaningful insights from it.

In particular, you can conceive data mining as some sort of pattern recovery task that you apply to a pool of data. Therefore, data mining will rely on classical and advanced components of Artificial Intelligence, pattern distribution systems and the traditional statistics that we have examined in the previous chapters.

Basic requirements of data mining
Any data mining process must incorporate the following components:

- Data warehouse
- Database Management Systems
- Online Analytical Processing (OLAP)
- Real-time analytics
- Data sources

Let's explore these components

#1: Data warehouse

A data warehouse is a core part of BI that stores and reports data analytics. Data warehousing underscores capturing of data from disparate sources for useful analysis and access. I know you're now thinking, "How is a data warehouse different from a database?"

While a data warehouse integrates data from diverse sources for the sole purpose of organizing them into a single coherent system for improved processing, a database contains only logical related and shared data. There are two approaches that you can apply to data warehousing. The top-down approach will spin off the data marts for specific groups of users when a complete data warehouse has been developed.

The bottom-up approach will build the database first and then combines it into a single, coherent system. In most cases, the data warehouse will be housed on an enterprise mainframe server system. In recent times, cloud computing has emerged as the key technology for hosting data warehouses where data from the different online transaction processing (OLTP) systems and other sources are selectively extracted for use.

#2: Database Management Systems

These are programs that can help you to process the data warehouse to mine important insights from data. The database management systems that you can use in a data warehouse are:

- IBM DB2 Warehouse
- Microsoft SQL Server
- Oracle Database 11g
- Teradata Enterprise Data Warehouse
- Sybase IQ
- Netezza Performance Server

#3: Online Analytical Processing (OLAP)

OLAP is used to perform multidimensional analysis of the business to provide the capability for complex computations, trend analysis, and even complex data modeling. It is the foundation for many types of business applications in business performance management, budgeting, forecasting, simulations models, knowledge discovery and data warehouse reporting. It allows the end-users of data mining to perform ad hoc analysis of data that exists in multiple dimensions to help them obtain helpful information that they can understand and use.

A corporate data warehouse or even a departmental data mart is useless if the data can't be put to use. The main goal of any data mining system is to help develop processes that ordinary employees can use in their jobs instead of relying on advanced statistical techniques. Similarly, the data warehouse and the information obtained from the mining process should be compatible across a broad spectrum of systems.

For this reason, products within the data mining arena should always evolve toward an easing of use and interoperability about systems in place. For all the data mining tools, it is vital to keep the business goals in mind when choosing and deploying tools. While putting these tools to use, it is helpful to examine where they will fit in the decision-making processes. The five steps in any data mining process are outlined below:

- Develop the standard reports.
- Identify the exceptions. These are the unusual situations and outcomes that show potential problems or advantages in data.
- Identify the causes of the exceptions.
- Develop mining models for possible alternatives.
- Track the effectiveness of the solutions.

Ultimately, you will generate standard reports for the normal database queries that inform how well the business is performing. When the exceptions occur, the details of the situation should always be available. You can either use data mining or develop hypotheses and test them using analytical tools such as OLAP. When you get your results, you can then test those using "what-if" scenarios which are easily available in programs such as Ms Excel.

#4: Real-time analytics
Using software applications, real-time analytics can help a business respond to customers in real-time based on the trends in the emails, messaging systems, and even the digital displays. Since all the information is being relayed in real-time, the business can use the data to

craft creative products that promote the bottom line of the organization. If a CEO is interested in tracking the time and location of their customers, he/she can easily interact with them using the data mining system in real-time.

#5: Data sources

This component of data mining involves the various forms of stored data. It is about taking the raw datasets and using the software applications to build meaningful data sources where each division can use to impact the business positively. Data scientists can use this strategy to create data tools that allow the data to be placed into a large cache of spreadsheets, pie charts, and tables for business purposes.

For instance, the dataset can be used to create presentations that structures attainable team goals. Looking at the strategic aspects of the data sources, you can make fact-driven decisions that take into account a holistic view of the needs of your organization.

Next up, let's explore the types of data mining techniques.

Types of data mining techniques

Raw data is not any different from the crude oil. Today, any person or institution with a moderate budget can collect large volumes of raw data. But the collection in itself shouldn't be the end goal. Companies that can extract meanings from the collected raw data are the ones that can compete in today's complex and unpredictable environment.

At the core of any data refinement process sits what we are referring to as "data mining techniques." Here are common data mining techniques:

- Descriptive
- Diagnostic
- Prescriptive
- Exploratory
- Predictive
- Mechanistic
- Casual
- Inferential

Let's dive in and explore these technologies.

#1: Descriptive analytics

The primary focus of descriptive analytics is to summarize what happened in an organization. Descriptive Analytics examines the raw data or content—that is manually performed—to answer questions such as:

- What happened in the organization?
- What is happening in the organization?

Descriptive data mining analytics is characterized by conventional business intelligence and visualizations such as the bar charts, pie charts, line graphs, or the generated narratives. A simple illustration of descriptive analytics can be assessing credit risk in a bank where the past financial performances help to predict client's expected financial performance. Descriptive analytics is useful in providing insights into sales cycle such as categorizing customers based on their preferences.

#2: Diagnostic analytics

As the name suggests, diagnostic data mining technique is used to unearth or to determine why something happened. For example, if you're conducting a social media marketing campaign, you may be interested in assessing the number of likes, reviews, mentions, followers or fans. Diagnostic analytics can help you distil thousands of mentions into a single view so that you can make progress with your campaign.

#3: Prescriptive analytics

While most data analytics provides general insights on the subject, prescriptive analytics gives you with a "laser-like" focus to answer precise questions. For instance, in the healthcare industry, you can use prescriptive analytics to manage the patient population by measuring the number of patients who are clinically obese.

Prescriptive analytics can allow you to add filters in obesity such as obesity with diabetes and cholesterol levels to find out areas where treatment should be focused.

#4: Exploratory analytics

Exploratory Analytics is an analytical approach that primarily focuses on identifying general patterns in the raw data to determine the outliers and other features that might not have been anticipated using other analytical types. For you to use this approach, you have to understand where the outliers are occurring and how other environmental variables are related to making informed decisions.

For example, in biological monitoring of data, sites can be affected by several stressors. Therefore, stressor correlations are vital before you attempt to relate the stressor variables and biological response variables. The scatterplots and correlation coefficients can provide you with insightful information on the relationships between the variables.

However, when analyzing different variables, the primary methods of multivariate visualization are necessary to provide greater insights.

#5: Predictive Analytics

Predictive analytics is the use of data, machine learning techniques, and statistical algorithms to determine the likelihood of future results based on historical data. The primary goal of predictive analytics is to help you go beyond just what has happened and provide the best possible assessment of what is likely to occur in future.

Predictive models use recognizable results to create a model that can predict values for different type of data or even new data. Modeling of the results is significant because it provides predictions that represent the likelihood of the target variable—such as revenue— based on the estimated significance from a set of input variables. Classification and regression models are the most popular models used in predictive analytics.

Predictive analytics can be used in banking systems to detect fraud cases, measure the levels of credit risks, and maximize the cross-sell and up-sell opportunities in an organization. This helps to retain valuable clients to your business.

#6: Mechanistic analytics

As the name suggests, mechanistic analytics allow big data scientists to understand precise alterations in procedures or even variables which can result in changing of variables. The results of mechanistic analytics are determined by equations in engineering and physical sciences. Also, they allow data scientists to identify parameters if they know the equation.

#7: Causal analytics

Causal analytics allow big data scientists to figure out what is likely to happen if one component of the variable is changed. When you use this approach, you should rely on some random variables to determine what's likely to happen next even though you can use non-random studies to infer from causations. This approach to analytics is appropriate if you're dealing with large volumes of data.

#8: Inferential analytics
This approach to analytics takes different theories on the world into account to determine the certain aspects of the large population. When you use inferential analytics, you'll be required to take a smaller sample of information from the population and use that as a basis to infer parameters about the larger population.

Data Mining Best Practices
The ultimate objective of data mining is to help the organization gain helpful information from large volumes of data. If you're planning to set up a data mining in your firm for improved processing and decision making, best practices in data mining can help you achieve your bottom line.

Here are best practices for data mining:

- Ensure that you have fully understood the reasons why data mining is being conducted in your organization. If the senior management wants data mining to unearth mundane information such the monthly sales figures, it may not be necessary to spend your time on expensive and time-consuming data mining. However, if the senior management wants you to determine when a customer ordered specific items on different channels, then data mining may make sense.
- Ensure that you have defined your goals and strategic objectives that the management wants to be developed. Which goals do you want to achieve

with data mining? Which questions need answers as a result of mining? Answering such questions will help you to define goals that meet the business objectives.

- Establish if you have the required raw data to use in data mining. In other words, ensure your data sources are reliable and relevant for the purpose you are setting to achieve. For instance, just having information about products, orders, and the customers may not be enough to justify investments in data mining. You need to have detailed customer profiles, order histories, and full website analytic data.

- Identify all your possible data sources. The raw data that you'll use may be originating from many sources. Is it originating from online analytics, e-commerce databases, and social media platforms and customer support logs or brick and mortar POS? Knowing the data sources will help you craft better strategies for integration purposes during data mining.

- Determine the various data warehouse solutions that will promote the firm's objectives. This is important because each solution and the architecture have its own features and restrictions. Understanding their potentials will help you determine how to use the tools to your advantage.

- Always define the level of security for your data. Data security is vital in any organization. Think about what the different security requirements that should be in place to get access to the data. Will data require encryption? Will you require a firewall or a backup system?

- Always implement the mining process in phases. Implementing the entire solution can take a longer time making you lose focus. Ensure that you prioritize your data mining needs and complete the process in stages.

- Always understand your data management strategy. When your company's use of data grows and changes, you may realize that some data becomes unusable. Constantly cleaning and confirming is much easier than a massive clean-u exercise. To avoid so many changes in your data, always monitor the database needs.

- Allocate the proper resources. Dealing with a data warehouse demands at least one full-time position. Activities such as maintenance, reporting, and validation are always ongoing. Having a full-time data manager makes sense.

Chapter 9: Final Thoughts on Data Analytics

Although we've focused on beginner topics for data analytics, there are still a lot of valuable tools that have emerged in recent times. Besides Ms Excel, you should try to learn at least one the following data analytic programming languages if you want to take your professional career to the next level:

- Python
- R
- MatLab
- Julia
- Hadoop
- Perl
- Julia

Strictly speaking, no language will fit all the analytic data problems. Each language has its own strengths and weaknesses. If you are an experienced programmer, I will advise you to start off with Python or R.

Besides learning these languages, it's important for me to mention that technology is changing fast. And really fast! Therefore, as a data scientist, there will always be some disruptive technologies coming on board to destabilize the conventional systems that you're familiar with. If there's one thing that's fueling the rise of these disruptive technologies, then it is big data.

In the recent past, organizations have been dealing with structured data which can easily be organized into tables and analyzed using the conventional RDBMSs. But today, firms are processing massive amounts of data that are either semi-structured or unstructured. To make matters worse, this data has a high velocity meaning that computational power has to increase.

At this rate, the conventional systems that you may be used to aren't sufficient.

In recent times, smart contracts have emerged as the future technology of analytics.

Smart contracts are program codes that can facilitate, execute, and enforce negotiations or performance agreements — Contract — using the Blockchain technology. These codes can act as substitutes for legal contracts where the terms of the contracts encoded in a computer programming language as a set of instructions.

The potential to link smart contracts to data analytics is perhaps one of the first steps towards creating a new world of opportunities. Now with advances in IoT that connect to cloud computing, wireless sensors and physical objectives that include small computer chips, smart contracts can provide these inanimate objects the level of artificial intelligence for data analytics in the 21st century.

But the use of smart contracts in these areas is yet to be seen. How the enforcement of smart contracts in code form and the prevailing laws and regulations in practice is still the greatest challenge that has to be resolved to realize the real potentials of smart contracts in data analytics.

Conclusion

Companies have had severe difficulties in harnessing their data into meaningful insights in the last couple of years. Because of skyrocketing volumes of data, today's interest in data analytics is unparalleled. While previous analysis centered on a few specific departments, today's analysis has to focus on all the departments of the organization.

Data analytics provides the only hope for fact-based and insightful-driven decisions that can help firms manage their strategic performance that can help them increase their shareholder value. That's why it's no longer tenable to ignore data analytics.

I hope that you've grasped all the basics of data analytics that you were looking out for in this book.

If you found this book useful, please take a moment to leave a review on Amazon as it'd greatly help us to improve our future ebooks for great customers like yourself!

Further Reading

Below are websites that can help you explore more about data analytics

https://www.sas.com

https://halobi.com/2016/07/descriptive-predictive-and-prescriptive-analytics-explained/

http://www.kdnuggets.com/2014/06/top-10-data-analysis-tools-business.html

http://www.informationbuilders.com/data-analysis

https://ori.hhs.gov/education/products/n_illinois_u/d atamanagement/datopic.html

http://www.bigskyassociates.com/blog/bid/356764/5-Most-Important-Methods-For-Statistical-Data-Analysis

http://www.thearling.com/text/dmwhite/dmwhite.htm

http://www.makeuseof.com/tag/create-free-survey-collect-data-excel/

https://oit.utk.edu/research/documentation/Document s/HowToUseExcelForDataEntry.pdf

https://www.skillsyouneed.com/num/statistics-identifying-patterns.html

http://homepages.rpi.edu/~bennek/class/mmld/talks/l ecture2-05.ppt

79426638R00043

Made in the USA
Columbia, SC
24 October 2017